Unique Euphony's

VOICES

A collection of poems

By Various Poets

Copyright© 2010

by Unique Euphony 24520-PIER

ISBN: Softcover 978-0-578-06286-0

All rights reserved. No part of this book may be reproduced or utilized in any form by any means, electronic or mechanical, including photocopying, recording, or by any information storage or retrieval system, without permission in writing from the publisher.

This book was printed in the United States of America

To Order additional copies of this book, contact:

Unique Euphony Publishing Group

1-706-577-3197

www.uniqueeuphony.com

inquiries@uniqueeuphony.com

Edit by Barbara Pierce

Cover Design by Chiara Richardson

Cover Illustration by Kirk Knox

Dedicated in Memory of... Samella Miller

Mommy Dearest

This is the hardest thing I've ever had to do

But I just had to write this special poem for you!!!

You have always been there for me through thick and thin.

When I felt as though I was going to lose

Your love was what helped me win...

Yes, you have always been there helped me endure my toughest times

Always showing you love me through all of my trials and crimes.

You made me a better person and that was not an easy thing to do.

Whenever I was scared and alone no one could comfort me, like you!!!

Mommy, I will always love you till the day that I die

Now you're gone, I'm lost and don't know what to do

But I must continue to live my life, and I do so in memory of you

So now that you've gone to go with God somewhere in time and space

Know that no one...no one could or would ever take your place

Mommy I miss you

Eddie "Quadir" Knox

CONTENTS

Voices..3

Chiara Richardson

Sometimes..6

A Poem at Age 24...8

Confessions of A Poet..9

Sheryl Haynes Williams

Bamboozled...14

Black Crow..16

Obesity...18

Death Be Kind...20

Even...22

Revelations 2000...24

Shaheen Darr

The Day When all Eyes Just Overflowed............28

Earth..30

Seasons of the Soul...32

The Dove..33

The Last Dance...34

The Road of Her Life..36

Georeen Tanner

The Branch is From the Tree..38

Brick by Brick..40

Now I Lay..42

Broad Street...44

Aaron Royer

God Knew..46

D's..52

The Answer of Love...54

God speaks When We Are Silent..57

I Am..60

Terry Lyle

The Path of the Storm...64

Alberta Harvey

My Fear..66

I Am...68

Our Cultural...69

Lonely..70

A Search for Peace...71

Eddie Stiles

When I Hear...74

That Ole Soul Inside..76

Tonza Sheree Thomas

I Am Not A Statistic..78

I'd Rather Start from the Bottom, Than Start from the Top........79

Sam Andras

A Childs Vision of the World..82

Aye

Choices..84

I Am Aye...86

Anti-Christ..88

Laura Lowe

The First Garden...92

Kirk Knox

School's in Session..96

School's in Session 2...98

Samuel Pittman

Wanna Provide..102

Eric Johnson

Long Concentrated Blinks..106

In My Momma's Eyes...107

Barbara "Muffin" Pierce

Remember When..110

Each and Every Day I Pray..115

Where Now...117

Just Think About It..118

Restless...121

Until I See You Again..122

VOICES

Listen real close to the **voices** you hear

the young, and the not so young of the twenty first century

who are surviving off power drinks for a source of energy.

Smoking a causal blunt to relax the move,

or as young people put it, the flow of things to come

like bringing down the house with dope spoken words.

A different type of poetic expression we use to call reading poetry.

Only spoken word gives more rhythm and rhyme.

This is another time when ole school doesn't control the new flow of words to be… **Voices** a loud demanding tone of harsh words makes you tremble to the fear of command. This is the introduction of a new meaning from the upcoming generation of this time… expressing the effects of many **voices**. **Voices** that express the different effects of words to be politically correct. Making words ear friendly, and teaching the facts of life. So hip, so cool, so smooth. Just listen to the words of young, and not so young… they have something to say, so hear the **VOICES…**

B. Muffin Pierce
© 2010

Chiara Richardson

Sometimes

Relationships spoil…like milk

You can smell it

Or tell it in the eyes

Or when the truth turns to lies

There aren't enough alley byes

Or la la byes to sing

But you will cling to those feelings

Before the expiration date expired

And you retired the I's for we's

Like we…

Used to be so happy

Then life sank her teeth in

Reality kicked in

And there was no defense

We both pleaded the fifth

Let the filth of society

Paint our expectations

Then 'I love yous'

Are spoken with reluctant hesitation

Forever just simply disappears

Like the need to want you here

Or the want to need you here

Or the ability to even hear you

Beyond these expectations

That ring loud like wedding bells

Or fairytales of happily ever afters

And after you…

I don't think I can love like this anymore

At least temporarily…

Or until some of these preconceived notions

Disappear like…

Pieces of you

Pieces of me and Forever

Just did.

A Poem at Age 24

Song turned to hummed melody

Dances more often solo

Skin begins to fit better

Accomplishments matter not

Life purpose swells

Fulfillment lurks around unexpected corners

Sorrow no longer an excuse

And love…

A passion

A pursuit

A pursuit to love me more at age 24

Confessions of a Poet

Life interrupting my dreams

Gotta seal my eyelids shut just so they won't fade

Hold fast to 'em

Clutch them near my heart

Pray they won't ever leave

Roll up my sleeve

This a fight I can't afford to loose

I did not choose these words

They chose me

To have, to carry, to marry

To be the barrier between the good and the bad

How sad…

They seem to be fading away

Can only pray

Dear Heavenly Father

Let not my living be in vain

These words are coursing through my veins

I breathe in and exhale them

You can smell them on my skin

They will not let me be

Not let me

Not let my living be in vain

Dear Heavenly Father

Let me live up to the expectations of being your daughter

A Sister, a lover, a friend, a poet

Let not my words be in vain

For they will remain the stains of my soul

Splattered upon your universe

When I can no longer rehearse this thing called life

So let me live

Let me live

Live bold and free

As the words that drip from my tongue

And resound like gongs off ears

I am here

Because of them

From my lips to my hips from my toes to hair follicles

They are me

Let me live as free

As the words that dance in my dreams

Let me live bold

As the hues that adorn your rainbows

Let me represent these words as they have me

And I pray I you

Sheryl Haynes Williams

Bamboozled

We been used, abused, accused and infused

By a justice that ain't blind.

We been misled, bred, bed and fed

On pity bread and poison wine.

So throw down the rope and let us climb.

The college ain't been built

To educate where we from.

The doctor to heal our pain

Ain't never been born.

So pass us the ball and let us run.

We been greeted, beated, cheated and mistreated

By the decisions of the mass.

We been blamed, framed, maimed and shamed

By a color-based ruling class.

So move out of the way and let us pass.

It'll take a million diaries

To hold the secrets we hide,

And a national act of contrition

Can't replace our stolen pride.

So slow down the chariot and let us ride.

Black Crow

In memory of my sister Nancy

Black crow don't bother me

Sitting up in that Georgia tree

Cawing loud and free

Feeding on my misery

Mocking the tears I hide

Fear and guilt mingled inside

Angry at the one who died

Taking the road instead of me

Piercing eyes never ending

Praying knees never bending

Anguished soul keep defending

Predestined plans of eternity

And to think you sit there grinning

As if in a race you are winning

Destroying the thoughts of new beginning

Beady, black eyes keep watching me.

But, I say oh crow of mine

Life is by choice and not design

So now I'll close my window blind

And wonder who will cry for me.

OBESITY

I watched her when she wasn't looking,

I saw the weary on her face.

She, for all the world to despise

Me, in my secret hiding place.

Her movement was lacking in rhythm,

Each step so labored with pain

But, she laughed loudest of all

As I sank deeper into shame.

Stop hurting us I begged,

When she refused to do right.

Then I watched the hands go round

As she tossed and turned all night

And I prayed for morning light.

She knew I was her prisoner,

Trapped many years by heartache

But, she couldn't free our spirit

Neither for mine nor pity's sake.

And every time she tried

A new routine or plan,

I was afraid to get excited,

Thinking she would fail again.

Fear crippled her every effort

With a promise she could not keep.

So, I waited in my hiding place

Until she fell fast asleep,

Then I began to weep.

Death Be Kind

Tribute to Michael Jackson

For you, the world was your stage,

For me, you were my world.

A silly, foolish, star-struck girl

Worshipping you like the angel you were named

With neither condemnation nor shame

Contending with the devil that made you blind.

Over the years, loving you became hard.

Though I rebuked the rumors, I shunned your face

Forgetting my childish devotion or the warm embrace

That you gladly bought to my carefree youth.

However, deep down I always knew the truth

Steeped in the recesses of my mind.

Yesterday, I heard on the evening news

That you had sadly passed away.

Somehow, I knew you weren't meant to stay.

Because as a child, you had to learn

To accept life on its cruelest terms

Surrounded by predators, the most dangerous kind.

So lay down your bourdons into our father's arms,

As he gently rocks you while you sleep,

And I'll renew the promise I did not keep.

To be a loyal and devoted friend

Cherishing your memories until the end

Now, Rest In Peace and let Death Be Kind.

EVEN

Tribute to the USA soldiers after 911

Eat even if you have no taste

Sleep even though you cannot rest

Fight even when crippled with fear

Tarry even if you fail the test

Smile even though you feel no joy

Speak even if you want to shout

Pray even though your faith is weak

Stand even when your strength gives out

Watch even though your eyes are tired

Endure even if you have to wait

Hope even when you feel no need

Love even in a time of hate

Give even though your funds are low

Sing even with a choking breath

Trust even if justice seems slow

Live even when facing death

Revelations 2000

Junkies wearing suits and ties

Making decisions on Capitol Hill

Unreal illusions on the catwalk

Phone psychics telling us how to feel

Love is just a bargaining tool

'Cause everybody's keeping it on the down-low

Our children are testing two steps behind

I think I'll get me a slow grind

Rap songs tell us to get a gun

Internet damn near rule the world

Brown skin children scared of the sun

I think I'll be a cover girl

Another cut-up body found today

They say the girl was only ten

No time to pray or reflect

Rush hour on, my turn next

Man down the street wearing a dress

I'm told he is the preacher's son

Sexy children's beauty contest

You know the end is soon to come

Shaheen Darr

The Day When All Eyes Just Overflowed……

A history like no other, a people like no other

From the blood of our forefathers sprang roots like no other

The darkness of our colour became our downfall

Perpetuated crimes against us to make us appalled

Silent struggles weighed heavy on shoulders strong

Only songs and poems revealed the blues, the wrongs

Men and women who dared to speak out and scream

Words of hope, words of change, words like "I have a dream"

Many died with no change in sight,

Never to be forgotten, they brought strength to our fight

As the years rolled by a people stood upright

Looked beyond the horizon, their futures bright

Black people proud, creativity in the depths of their soul

Found themselves, finally got their lives in control

And amongst them a rare diamond was being slowly polished

Behind the scenes waiting one day to establish

That being black was beautiful and black could rule

The day finally came when the world stood still to watch this jewel

A black man became the most powerful man in the world

And that was the day when all eyes just overflowed

The ancestors lay in the grounds and closed their eyes

Their fight was complete, time to rest, time to say goodbye

Restless spirits found peace in their hearts

Their blood was not wasted; this was only the start....

Earth

As I lie down on the carpet of soft green grass,

I look up at the branches of the oak looming above me

Her protective branches hide the clouds as they pass

Playing hide and seek as if in the clear blue sea

And then I see the fallen leaves of yesteryear

Dry and crisp, lifeless at the feet of their tree

Death has not spared them it would appear

Its finger has touched them as meant to be

Sadness overwhelms me as I think of earth

A virgin once, young and full of promises

Lush, fertile, rich, and so full of worth

Waiting to grow, waiting for new enterprises

Through the years as men became corrupt

Wanted more and more, gave less and less

All that was natural on Earth did they disrupt

She started to change, she began to stress

Under her silent surface, her blood began to boil

No more tears, now they started to dry

Feeling ravaged she only felt recoil

It was as if she gave up and wanted to die

I put my face against the soft grass and cried

Mother earth, forgive us, and give us another chance

Only silence around me, but the wind did sigh

My cheeks were wet as the sun set in the distance.........

Seasons of the soul

New beginnings, a spring like season arrives

Human birth, a seedling in the garden of life

Childlike innocence, eyes crystal clear, untouched

Taking first steps, discovering what the world is about

Discovery continues, awareness abounds

As summery days get fuelled with the energy of youth

Too many distractions leave no time for reflection

The passing of time seems to go unnoticed

All summer days have to come to an end

When the winds of autumn start to blow

The soul now starts to reflect, on times gone by

Bodies that never tired, now ask for help

The winter chill never felt this cold before

Bones never felt this weak before

The soul, too tired to remember its past

Now sits in the dark, awaiting its new chapter……

The Dove

The clouds of dust cleared and through the burning rubble

I saw destruction straddling the once peaceful land so green

What had taken men years to build and to nurture

Now lay broken, twisted and unrecognizable

I heard cries of men, women and of children

Cries that questioned, cries that made me tremble

Lives had no meaning that fateful day

When destruction reigned as king for that day

As my dazed eyes looked at this scene so dreadful

A speck of white I saw on the horizon

A dove, untainted and untouched flew regardless

Its journey had to go on even as the world wept

A peaceful, silent messenger flew above the rest

I wished I too could fly to where she flew

I wished I too could be oblivious to it all like she was......

The Last Dance

Like the candle burns bright just before it dies

One last flash hoping to regain its dimming light

Leaves too perform a last dance

And herald a new season with flamboyance

Winds remind them of colder days to come

Gently coaxing so they willingly succumb

And let go of mothering branches that held them so

That saw them bud that saw them grow

Defiance takes the reigns, time to take over the show

The gentle, the shy leaf to exist no more

No more to be the same, to be so uniform

Time to bring out the self, to just perform

Out come the reds, out come the maroons,

Like the butterfly springing from the cocoon

No time to stay in the shade

They even wear gold for this parade

Everywhere you look, colour abounds

It makes you gasp it makes you turn around

The show is on, watch this one before it goes

This is their last dance in death's throes

Fallen they lie in their thousands

At the feet of the silent giants

Their red colour taints the dark earth

Their death prophesying a new birth

The Road of her life

The road ahead of her seemed wide and welcoming

A mirage cleverly created by a master illusionist

Confused she stopped in her tracks

There was still time to turn back, her footsteps to retract

Hoping for some advice, for some words of wisdom

No friends about, just her mind, her body, her soul

She knew this road had to be traversed

Its outcome to bear, for better or for worse

As the trees cast their long shadows in the sunset

The woman slowly started to walk the long road

Only once she turned her face to look back

The large sad eyes as if saying a final farewell

The cold wind seemed to nudge her back

But no turning back, she had chosen her own track

The lone figure walked the road into the sunset

The shadows lengthened as if to cover her footsteps…..

Georeen Tanner

The Branch is from the Tree

I snuggled close to her

Not so much for affection

But for protection

She held me tight

As you held the mirror above your head

Screaming out the hate upon which you fed

Years later in your car

You ranted and raved

About the woman whose chest I caved

In fear of you

Now you are eager to know

Why I treat you as a foe

You must understand

I love you dearly

But I hate how yearly

You call me with a woe-is-me-story

It's gory

To hear you say you love me

For how can you love me the branch

And not her the tree?

Brick by Brick

I am Newark,

your unproud whore

the good time gal you'll never take home

you talk about me you laugh about me

pretend around me that you love my "urban charm"

say you only want what's best

while my sun starved children hide under their beds

praying the bulletstorm stops

my streets are littered with your wide-eyed gasps

at my close-mouthed good mornings, at my pit bull saunters

I see you shaking on a deal

lining me with Broad and Market cop cars

hoping no one will stick a pin in your painted facelift

I taste your whispers

you say I wallow in fried chicken, ketchup, and french fries

for breakfast

—with a gum wad side.

you say I wash it all down with Passaic spit streams

wipe my mouth with a rat behind 99 cent curtains

watching the thugs go by

close your eyes when you kiss me

loan me to your pearly pal

let them see the sights as '67 riots rage inside

they won't see my despairing sparrow tears

you'll powder them with pseudo-Samaritan make-up

Now I Lay

January icicles form under tracks

home to pigeon droppings I duck between

waiting patiently for the green for a chance

to relive that vrooming auto mechanic shop

with the little black puppy I never pet

because I was scared to cross the street.

That's where the sky lit up

like so many Independence Days

when guys stole cars from out of town,

did a donut, struck a match, and fled the scene.

I sat right in that second story window

elbows on the sill, mouth gaped; eyes fired orange, yellow, red.

The lady above me had her mouth gaped, too

since her husband was beating her

every Saturday night with the salsa tunes and

hard boots that boom boom boomed in my sleep.

1010 WINS gave me the world every 7 am

when it was just a one bedroom and an unwritten child support check

that shoved a boy into manhood and made a girl dream of diamond stars

as they prayed the Lord their souls to take.

Broad Street

Sidle through the park and you'll see

the men in their white tees

jumpin jacks at eight

that ain't seen

a woman in five to ten

their eyes will lick your frame

as you stumble past

a needle marked doctor who needs a quarter and a fix

to the right of the bodega where

one, two, three crying babies cling

to a bare legged lady whose

ends ran coasts apart when

her happily ever after split

like the banana reality of the kid on the corner

with his hand on a 45 that goes off before he can blink

Aaron Royer

God Knew

Tissue rescues my face

As pride subsides from the pollutions of sin

The same evil that once destroyed the world before

We have a history that can become history

Hate once filled my eyes and ears

In the struggle love still finds a way to prevail

I was close but God never let me give up

On life even though death seems somewhat easier

Someone not something was calling me

Thou the sand of time maybe calling our body

Our Spirit wants to be free

Free of the evil that covers it

Flesh, sin seems to embedded in our skin

I feel for those newborns

Who cry because of their first evil taste?

Because of evil's stench

Even as babies we are already running

Daily being stalked by our adversary

Hunted because our souls have a chance

Daily we seem to be sent to wolves

Wolves dressed in sheep's clothing

Daily the news is telling the season and time

Temptation seems to waiting at our door steps

We run but cannot hide

From the evil, but we can rebuke it

Like Jesus did in the wilderness

Evil wants to devour the righteousness

We have left to do good for next the generation

In these times God said He will never leave nor forsake us

I remember my question

Do I run to the living tree or the Tree of Life?

Where the branches stretch past forever

Protecting us from evil rain

God answer was simple

Come and sup with me,

Take a step toward love

Before I could say Sorry

God said I know and read my file

His hand reached down

Handing me a cup engraved with words

Drink of my life, Take my Joy, and Take my strength

Wolves dressed in sheep's clothing

Daily the news is telling the season and time

Temptation seems to waiting at our door steps

We run but cannot hide

From the evil, but we can rebuke it

Like Jesus did in the wilderness

Evil wants to devour the righteousness

We have left to do good for next the generation

In these times God said He will never leave nor forsake us

I remember my question

Do I run to the living tree or the Tree of Life?

Where the branches stretch past forever

Protecting us from evil rain

God answer was simple

Come and sup with me,

Take a step toward love

Before I could say Sorry

God said I know and read my file

His hand reached down

Handing me a cup engraved with words

Drink of my life, Take my Joy, and Take my strength

Wolves dressed in sheep's clothing

Daily the news is telling the season and time

Temptation seems to waiting at our door steps

We run but cannot hide

From the evil, but we can rebuke it

Like Jesus did in the wilderness

Evil wants to devour the righteousness

We have left to do good for next the generation

In these times God said He will never leave nor forsake us

I remember my question

Do I run to the living tree or the Tree of Life?

Where the branches stretch past forever

Protecting us from evil rain

God answer was simple

Come and sup with me,

Take a step toward love

Before I could say Sorry

God said I know and read my file

His hand reached down

Handing me a cup engraved with words

Drink of my life, Take my Joy, and Take my strength

You are The All Knowing Father

Thanks for sending the Deliver Jesus

Tears are not a sign weakness

Tears are a sign of passion and resolve

Compromise is a sign weakness

Remember God knows you

Our Choices are the author of our life story

God knew us as a Friend, Glory

D's

We are taught to get A's in school

Because excellence we were told has promise

First understand the mistakes that equaled those D's

That's when the process of change begins

Then we can rise above them to get our A's

For God is stilling working in us and for us

Bringing us closer to His plan of completion

Find your why definition

Find your love, passion and means of devotion

Love the fact that you're different

Be thankful for those harsh yet fair disciplines

That taught us honor, virtue and integrity

Giving us personality, responsibility, purpose driven life possibilities

Straightening our priorities as we accept our personal call of duty

We have to get pass the distractions

Diversions of costly time wasting deceiving attractions

To many are being disconnected from their families and communities

Like those in the bible who had leprosy

Let's search for the real High Priest and say thank you

Only Jesus can deliver us, bless us and heal us while giving us mercy

Decreasing our pride increases our chances of obtaining our goals

Dreams are not limited unless we forgot who gave us them

Destiny rises like the sun over the horizon

Desire should help us get there

Influencing us to make prosperous decisions

God's love and strength already gave us the determination

Our faith confirms how, where we live

Question is which D's do you see when you look in the mirror

The Answer of Love

It searches and calls us together

Deep and wide devoting time

Staying close to our side

Tickling our lips to smile

Picking us up while we kneel

Seals the deal of true happiness

It answers our questions

Changing musical notes to words

Forgives and heals the broken

Tastes sweeter than honey

Making us richer than money or gold

Inspires a deeper and greater closeness

It makes Fairy Tales

Become true stories in our reality

Intimacy trembles more than our greatest orgasm

Passionate, love lights its own fire

Creating a safe path through the shadows

Holds strong when our ground shakes

It is God Himself

Jesus died and rose for it purpose

Dances with us, caresses our whole being

Encourage us to face our fear

Of loyalty, honesty and trust unconditionally

Embracing fidelity as we share faith

It is the rope of hope

Cures the poisonous bite of hate

Universally speaking in one true voice

Love always knows our name

Stopping time just to take pictures

Giving us memories through our lifetime

It's God's Love that stays and never leaves us

Help, change and reveal the new us

Fly free, crown us, surround us

Life means nothing to us without it

Let love precious keys open new doors

God Speaks When We Are Silent

We all dream about a creating masterpiece

While we investigate our rich histories

Only collaboration on get rich schemes

Demonstrating our underlined skills and values

Delegating powers for love and for fame

Liberating our false rights and freedoms

Until our Miranda Rights are quoted

Then we plead the fifth proudly

Now we are a prisoner of our very own words

The problem doesn't always start with our mouths

It starts with our ears; still no one seems to listen

Until triggers, fire blazes and bullets fly

Because of untold stories called "I am sorry"

Your move or do you want stay at this stalemate

Between missed opportunities and wasted time

Our vision is never disabled

As we shoot for our silver star in life

Until we stumble or fail

Rising saying star backwards rats

This is only the beginning of success

Sadly some choose the bitter end called insanity

As words is exchange repeatedly

Expected difference when our yesterday's equals today's

Throwing stones at our own glass houses

I'm telling you problems start in our ears

Suppose we had to eat everything we said

Immediately we would think before we speak

Sometimes it is good to pause

Be silent, be still and think

Most importantly listen

God is speaking to you

God would never give you keys

If He didn't intend for you to use them

To open your house or to come home,

It is better to get an ear infection

While listening to knowledge and wisdom

Than to get one because we didn't listen at all

Usually big things grow from something small

Too many have missed the call and wonder why they fall

Some people only hear hummingbirds behind walls

And that's their moment of freedom as bird calls

The abuse of words sometimes equals the absence of life

God spoke things into existence

His very image is why we exist

Our words have power

But so do our ears

Listening to our ancestors

Someone has done and been there before

God is our oldest ancestor

Listening to God himself

I think makes a lot of sense

It just takes a moment

Just listen, God speaks when we are silent

I Am

I am nothing

Without the Great I AM

The voice of reason and thanks

The rejoice in the songs of freedom

Honoring those that paved the way

I am the aftermath

Of pain through labored love

The son of a great Mercedes

Who shifted and transferred

Now rides among the clouds R.I.P

I am the result of pressure

Those precious coals before me

Leaving those priced diamonds after me

The example of a miracle before

And messenger of good news after

I am the thought that made sense

More than my height, age, weight, race and location

More than the application and resume reads

Truly the evidence of love

Successful through the element of forgiveness

I am the failure

That chooses to change

To encourage success

That understands life is not promised

That death weeps through its witnesses

I am words that punch

That leaves no pain

As memories remind me why tears fell

Worda once touched my heart

I am the hello salutations

Never wanting to say Good bye

Give God all the Glory not me

Lets say see you later

In heaven next to the Great I AM

Terry Lyle

The Path of the Storm

The sky was dark blue, and approaching across the horizon were storm clouds. I wondered how bad was this going to be, will the storm pass over? Within minutes, a constant pounding against my window pane was thumping loudly as if an intruder was trying to get in.

Huddled beneath my blankets, I trembled as my lights began to flicker, with the loud emergency sirens blaring in the distance. How long would the storm last? How long would it devastate everything in its path?

A cold eerie silence came upon the room. Then in an instant, a flash of blinding lightning filled the room, followed by a crackling and rumbling of thunder. The hairs on my neck became prickly, because of my fear of the storm. All alone and frightened, I began to pray for sleep, so I could ride out the storm peacefully in my slumber.

I scrambled to find a sleeping pill because the tension intensified. I'm not sure of whether there will be extensive damage to my home or injuries to myself because I was caught in the path of the storm. Loud thunder rumbling and lightning illuminating the room in its scary brightness, as car horns were going off and strong gusty sounds of the wind blew outside, knocking things around against my home.

As I listened to the emergency sirens going off in the distance, I wondered why I didn't heed the evacuation warnings that were made all day long. I didn't listen and now I find myself stuck in the path of the storm. I thought I would be brave enough to stay so I could watch my possessions, which I now find underwater, as I scramble to the roof. I hope someone will be brave enough to venture out to find me, while I am stuck in the path of the storm.

Alberta Harvey

My Fears

Fear is the emotion I experience most

I fear how people see me most of all

I want them to see me as I see myself

But it is others who say who I am

I fear how well I am doing on my job

If I lose my job how would I support myself?

How would I deal with the feeling of failure?

I fear poor health not being able to take of myself

I fear the burden that this would put on someone else

I fear closed-in places, especially elevators

The walls seem to want to close in on me

I fear large crowds this mass of flesh invades my personal space

I fear meeting strangers because first impressions are lasting

I fear aggressive behavior because anger leaves emotional scars

I fear loneliness not having someone to talk to when I need to talk.

I fear stormy weather it feels like the world is out of control.

I fear freeways but I drive them in order to get where I need to go.

I have a fear of water but I want to learn to swim

I fear I will hurt someone or be rejected if I express myself

Even though I would like to say how I feel.

My fears tighten my stomach and increase my breathing

My mind is so cloudy then my thoughts turn to God

He did not give me this spirit of fear

So then I can say I will not be afraid.

I Am

Born of love and grace divine

Of human pride and painful cry

A human face!

Born of dust and spoken breath

Of powerful will and mournful soul

A human heart!

Born of flesh and eternal spirit

Of thoughtful mind and prayerful hands

I Am…

Our Cultural

Covers our American and African Heritage

Unites us in a bond of dignity and unity

Let's these bonds build our community

Tells us who we are and where we are going

Uncovers our talents, gifts, knowledge and faith

Reminds us of our social skills and struggles

Accepting our culture empowers our lives

Loving yourself is the key to a joyous life!

Lonely

The lonely nights are passing by

I'm watching the stars up in the sky

I know that you are watching too

That's why my nights are sad and blue

The stars are full and far apart

I feel the same within my heart

A tear from my eye begins to fall

I will this night, I shall not cry

For I remember the joy, just you and I

My love for you will never die!

A Search for Peace!

Free my body

Free my mind

Free my soul

Free me from this agony

In my hands lies the means

To free me from this painful life

There are no words

That can express this deep despair

So no one will hear my silent plea

But in my hands lies the means

To set me free and give me peace

God has heard and will forgive this

act of will…

Eddie Stiles

WHEN I HEAR

When I hear a new born cry,

    I'm reminded of my birth into slavery.

When I hear the rustles of dry leaves,

    I'm reminded of the long summer days in the cotton fields.

When I hear the cracking of wood burning,

    I'm reminded of crosses on fire in the front lawn.

When I hear the popping of leather in air,

    I'm reminded of the brutal bare-back-beatings administered

    by overseers

When I hear the wind blow and whistle a tune,

    I'm reminded of the songs that kept oppressed souls going.

When I hear the rattling of chains,

    I'm reminded of shackles, leg-irons, and the flesh that they tore from ankles and wrists.

When I hear a door open,

    I'm reminded of master coming into the shacks at night to take my mother or my sister and maybe me or my brother.

When I hear the white folks gather in town,

    I'm reminded of the auctions of my black people.

When I hear the breeze flow through the trees,

    I'm reminded of the black fruits that hang from the branches.

When I hear all these things,

    I'm reminded of the time I want to forget...

        ...SLAVERY

That Ole Soul Inside

That ole soul inside never lets me down

it always seem to have a smile

when I'm stuck with a frown.

When I am mean, it is nice

supporting me with great advice.

Some people call it a sixth sense

I say its clairvoyance.

It's a deep inner feeling

so real, strong and revealing.

I'm often asked "why it chose me?"

Only to be told it's the powers that be!

I prayed for it to go away

only to find out it's here to stay.

I promised myself I'll always trust, listen and confide

to the voice of that ole soul inside.

Tonza Sheree Thomas

I AM NOT A STATISTIC

It took me awhile to figure out what I wanted to be and 8 months dropped out got a G. E. D. cause I had 2 little girls looking back at me.

I love what my mother provided because it brought me stability but I always wanted my daughters to be better than me! No projects, no stamps, no welfare for my crew so a sista had to do what a sista do. Beatin', battered and being shoved out of cars. I knew way back then that I could live through the scars. Blood, sweat & tears threw all of those years. I knew that if I made it I true-ly way his...

Several years later I returned to school, had 4 mouths to feed who was I tryna to fool? TANF running out & I were feeling full of doubt so I went to the Tech and GOD worked it out. The devil attached my home had my children acting grown but it didn't phase us we kept it moving on. Got the shackles off my feet, had to be all I could be cause in from of the kidz... I had to practice what I preached!

My kidz made me do it, it brought peace in my life & I said that once I made it I'd pass that light. "I AM NOT A STATISTIC" cause the Southside is in me, P.B.L. and S.S.L.C. gave me to the NAACP. Hot off the press and straight from the dome, this here business is home grown!

I thank my folks cause what I do, I do for you,

I'd Rather Start from the Bottom, Than Start from the Top

I'd rather start from the bottom than start from the top.
To appreciate what I ain't while I ain't got.
This life is a gamble you win or you lose.
Don't be the one getting caught pressing snooze.

Dayz come and dayz go and it happens real fast.
It seems like just yesterday I was walking through class.
Nothing on my mind but keeping up with the fads.
"Super sonic motivating these rhymes are creating".
But there were much bigger dreams ole' girl started to chasin'.
16 years old and thought I knew it all; fast as I got up I started to fall.
And there was only one name I had to call, Ma.

I'd rather start from the bottom than start from the top.
To appreciate what I ain't while I ain't got.
This life is a gamble you win or you lose.
Don't be the one getting caught pressing snooze.

Guess what, what, what? I got caught in a rout.
Momma alwayz told me to keep down my skut.
What you lookin' for gonna hit you dead in the ah...
Baby 1, baby 2 and then baby 3 but that's alright they all belong to me.
On me my seeds you can depend. Don't put your trust in a man.
I'm not tryna put yall down but due what you can.

I'd rather start from the bottom than start from the top.
To appreciate what I ain't while I ain't got.
This life is a gamble you win or you lose.
Don't be the one getting caught pressing snooze.

Sam Andras

A Childs Vision of the World

To take the time to step away,
from my world into hers.
To see through eyes with younger dreams,
I feel emotions stir.
With wonder and with innocence,
she asks "who paints the sky"?
"You know" I say "who it is",
then "God" is her reply.
I ponder on this question,
so young, pure honesty.
How deep, what beauty she must see,
uninhibited, truly free.
I see that I get drawn away,
those things I have to do.
But freedom comes when I can see,
a heart so pure and true.
For through those eyes I see the world,
so wonderful and free.
A world that shares its love and joy
in each discovery.

Aye

CHOICES

Life is but a series of choices

So Aye choose to be Light

And love my darkness

I choose to be free

Living within me

I choose to happy instead of sad

I choose not to let things that

I cannot change make me mad

I choose to exist above this physical plane

I choose that all I desire is mine to claim

I choose to love and not to hate

I choose to reside within Heaven's gate

I choose not to be food for negative energy

I choose to focus on positivity

I choose creativity so that I may choose my destiny

I choose to be rich instead of poor

I choose to be a Woman and not a whore

I choose to be eternal and not to burn in this life's inferno

I Am Aye

I am woman

And it is not easy you see

Because all that is depends on me

I am the bearer of seeds

I am the provider of needs

I am the Earth beneath your feet

I am the sky above your head

It is I who wrote the book of the dead

I am the Daughter of Rah

I am the Daughter of Mah

I am the essence of love and the enemy of hate

I am the words of wisdom standing at the city's gate

I am the truth that is enlightenment

I am the strength that holds the covenant

I am the mother of nations

It was I who created this devastation

It is I who gave birth to the holy prophets and appointed the Anointed ones

It is I who gave them the message of oneness so that you,

My most precious and beloved offspring could over come wickedness

And yet it is I that man has labeled as the wicked one

Recognize and realize that it is I that stood at his

Almighty side when the Earth project first begun

And it is He who has appointed yes me to be the one

I am Aye

Anti-Christ

Stop trying to re program me

Do not try to delete the original seed

With your lies of what was and what will be

Trying to recreate a book in history

And call it prophecy

I know your deep hidden secret

It is your power, your claim to Glory

So why is it that you are afraid to tell the whole story?

Sold humanity for silver and gold

Persecute all maintained The Way of Old

Claimed Divine Authority

Crucified Christ for heresy

Yet your "Divine Institution" commits heresy every day!

Proclaim yourselves the superior race

Yet you don't appear to see that you have fallen from grace

Blinded by your fame and riches

Preaching and teaching lies

A House divided will not stand

You can not serve two masters

For you will love one and hate the other

The Deceiver has died! In case you didn't know

Repent or be destroyed!

Yes his descendents live

But the age of the Ram Has long been over

Now his spell will be broken

And your "Divine Institution" will fall

Jews, Muslims, Buddhist and Christians

Will no longer separate themselves

We choose no one religion, we choose no one tradition

We choose no one god over the other

We choose The Divine Source of ALL that Was, ALL that Is,

ALL that Will BE!

And here on Earth, We claim that which is ours,

By the Divinity of Adam & Eve and the promise that was made to their seed

The right to live and rule our planet by the rules of Humanity

Not animal brutality

The Truth will be known to ALL eventually

This is reality, repent now and give birth to peace

The seed is ripe, labor pain will be great

But there is no purer moment of love than when

A mother gives birth!

Laura Lowe

The First Garden

Dear Mother, I miss you in every season
but in the spring I miss you more.

As for your departing, sometimes I forget the reason...
yet I cannot linger long for the garden is in need of the yearly chore.

Dear Mother, I see you in your garden of the spring
as you genuflect in the age old ritual of the mysterious union of seed and soil.
I dream myself in the garden of my soul as I hear the nightingale sing.
Come morning when the eastern fire is lit, the garden always,
forever awaits my daily toil.

Dear Mother, I wonder with a child's delight,
as I behold the wondrous beauty brought forth from the land.
Do you have a magic genie of the night?
Or is this the work of your hand.

My dear Mother, did you always know?
The answer is in the spring. It is a simple plan.

God's hand in our hands continually shows
We must never fail to recreate the first garden of the land.

Kirk Knox

School's in Session

School's in session, so open ears to these lessons.

In the past I was stressin', now I'm positively progessin'

I'm never restin' this blessin'.

I won't settle for less than the best, and you know that's right

These words are tight, so maybe you might

catch this spiritual spill

These words real...

sinkin' deep like oil drills

and verbal skills

flow like black gold

God planned my stay before the world unfold

so you can't control this natural born leader

Yes I be a seeker of knowledge

I've been to college

and I'm schooled in street life

Made mistakes that can break for a degree in strife.

Truth cuts like a knife

when you've lived a lie

We go through the motions, and never ask why

Some willing to die

for causes unknown

and allow foul acts within the homes we roam.

If you don't use your dome

to hold your own

In your sector,

you strive for body bags, or criminal collectors.

I betcha that only the strong survive,

so if you want to stay alive and free,

you must flee,

but not from your city, but from your current mind frame

cause where ever the area the struggles the same

Unless you change the game.

that keeps the brain stressin'

You'll settle for less than the best

and you won't count your blessings

So never end the lessons.

School's in Session Part 2

From neonate to necro

you should know that school's in session

and where there's a mistake

there too lies a lesson.

I'm guessin' that this is the way;

the things I've learned in my life I display,

I once portrayed the image of a Spiritualist,

but my walk wasn't serious

because I flipped the word like it was worthless.

Now, my purpose is to climb with divine reason

this is my season, but once I was freezin'

in a cold and lifeless winter

and now I'm about to enter

the warm sunrays of spring,

so check out the knowledge that this word brings

I sing a song of plenty for many from one

I won't stop 'til it's done,

because I'm spittin' my callin'
I once fell below bottom and now he's lifted what had fallin'.
It can't be any stallin' to receive his blessings and just remember
that school's always in session.

Samuel Pittman

Wanna Provide

I wanna provide for my baby

To expel the word lazy

I'm broke on child support, and

The situation seems crazy

At least from my perspective

In this world my pen and

Mentality is the only weapon

Preparation for arms to combat

The global recession

Enrolled in school late so

I must ketchup with the lesson

Only to provide for my daughter

Only to have this one option

Succeed…or lead her on the path

To financial slaughter.

I pray it gets better…meanwhile we

Must embrace weather

Together we're apart

Today, tomorrow will be

Joined , I pray

P.S. Aniya…I'm gonna

Save you one day.

Eric Johnson

Long Concentrated Blinks

...Got me enjoying this visual shadow hour

There's no such thang as night

Daylight is your smile...racing from your personality

The reality of you is moonfully illuminated in my mind

The only time I can enjoy your shine...

without being blinded by emotions

Coasting is attention along tides of my attraction

controlled by memories

I'm scared to open my eyes because you may not be there

to give your warmth and energies

Closed eyes keep you in my presence and I don't have to think

You're always in my dreams...

also known as...long...concentrated...blinks

In My Momma's Eyes...

I am the sun that rise and sets

I am the surprise in her life that she'll never forget

My brilliant light...keep her eyes shining with joy...my accomplishments makes her mouth drop

My warmth keeps her proud of me

I am the reflection in her eyes... that make tears drop

Barbara "Muffin" Pierce

Remember When?

i remember when i was a poet,

back then, when...

welfare was a way of living

sex was a sin

and santa claus, a friend ?

then

i was black and proud

james brown was singing loud

jesus christ was hanging

and the word was war

gil scott heron preaching

"the revolution will not be televised"

hot pants, halter tops

and afro wigs

disco fever

superfly

give me five, on the black hand side

i bet you don't know

curtis blow

john doe

give me some more

ree-fer...

negro please

black eye peas, food stamps

it's the first of the month

baby crying

momma please

don't hit me no more

i'll sleep on the floor

kool aid, kool aid

taste great,

wish i had some

can't wait.

winstons taste good

like a cigarette should

one, two, three... red light

uptight outa sight

i'll walk a mile for a camel

kiss my ass

i love you too

digging in the scene with the

gangster lean

pork and beans

black power

soul sister

ain't to proud to beg

before elvis was dead

ku klux klan

martin luther king

president kennedy just got shot

aunt Jemima's head still wrapped

jackson five

saturday night live

riots in the watts

racism ?

say it loud

i'm black and i'm proud

bell bottoms

coney island

double dutch bust

ready or not

here i come

rum and coke

and dirty jokes

my momma's boyfriend

ple-ase

my grandma and your grandma

was sitting by the fire

my grandma told your grandma...

i had a dream about fish last night

bright, damn near white

gold teeth, bare feet

record player

nigga hate-r

if you holler

let 'em go

eeny, meeny, miny mo

joe, i don't need you

any more

what's going on ?

platform shoes

singing on the corner

drinking wine

having a good time

fine

segregation

education

motivation

communication

back then

remember when?

peace...

Each and Every Day I Pray

It brings tears to my eyes when I see our young people

on the corners selling drugs to make ends meet.

While Mommy's at home watching the young and the restless,

and daddy's in the federal penitentiary.

Each and every day I pray for that child's safety.

I pray for that grandma who has worked her fingers to the bone

to feed her own children,

and now she's expected to raise her grandchildren.

Each and every day I pray for that grandma.

Each and every day I pray for the homeless children, and

for the teacher who has not been taught to understand the future,

or the preacher who doesn't reach out to the youth.

The father who hasn't paid his child support,

and the village that is no longer raising children.

I pray for the senseless gang banging among the youth,

and why won't you pull up your pants?

"God please grant me the serenity to change the things I could."

To educate the uneducated, to rid the drugs, and prevent teen pregnancy.

To take momma from the TV, and give grandma a vacation,

and when is daddy getting out of the penitentiary?

God thank you for your caring and your mercy,

and for that grandma, and bring back that village,

and let's educate our children.

Each and every day I pray for justice.

Where Now?

My life seems so different

from what it did ten years ago.

I am older, and much wiser

I've learned a lot

I've been many places

I've met many people

I've cried, and I've laughed

I've been sick

I've been depressed

I've been weak,

and I've been strong.

I've been used and abused,

but I've also had a good time.

Most of the time I've been honest,

and all the time I have faith,

and now that I've realized

where I've been

where do I go from here ?

Just Think About It...

If Rosa Parks didn't take that seat,

or Martin Luther King didn't dare to dream.

If James Brown didn't "Say it loud,.."

To make us realize we are black and proud.

Just think about Central High School that day in Little Rock, or

the first black family to move on the block.

The signing of the Emancipation Proclamation, and

becoming a great interim of this nation.

Sacrificing lives for freedom and justice

in order for us to have the right to vote.

Think about Medger Evers, Malcolm X, and

other black men and women brutally murder.

They gave their lives to open doors for us...

Just think about every time

you walk in the front door,

sit in the front seats of the buses,

and the movie theaters.

Your freedom to vote,

shop where you want to shop,

and to have the opportunities to be educated.

Just think about having the first

black President of the United States of

America, The land of opportunity.

Just think about George Washington Carver, and the peanut,

Garrett Morgan, and the traffic light.

Dr. Charles Drew exploring plasma.

The contributions of great Black Men and Women,

whom inventions and creations enhanced opportunities.

Just think back when we were Africans,

brought from our homeland to become Negroes on

unfamiliar grounds.

We were sold as coloured servants, and then

we were freed only to become Black and that wasn't enough,

so now we are called African American.

" Les not forget" the struggles that our fore fathers and mothers fought, in order for us as a people to move forward.

Pause for moment and think about it... think about it... Just think about it.

Restless

I closed my eyes to fall to sleep,

but I'm restless, and short of a dream.

I tossed and I turned

I tossed and I turned

I heard voices from the TV,

then I heard silence.

I made a trip to the toilet,

and went for a glass of water.

I returned and watched TV

I can't fall asleep

I turned on the light

and than I write...

good night

Until I See You Again

My dad died before I could see him one last time.

I wasn't able to tell him good-bye,

but until I see him again, I cry.

There was an old woman, who was a friend of mine,

and over time I grew quite fond of her.

I heard that she wanted to see me before she died,

but I didn't get the chance to say good-bye,

so until I see her again, I cry.

My mom died after I seen her one more time

My grieving for her is so intense

although I didn't have the chance to say good-bye,

One day, I'll see her again, and

until then, I cry.

CPSIA information can be obtained
at www.ICGtesting.com
Printed in the USA
FFOW01n1544150115
10210FF